ADJECTIVES & ADVERBS

A Remedia Publication

Illustrated by Danny Beck

ISBN #1-56175-118-9

REMEDIA PUBLICATIONS   **10135 E. VIA LINDA, #D124**   **SCOTTSDALE, AZ 85258**
Toll Free 1-800-826-4740   **FAX 602-661-9901**

TABLE OF CONTENTS

ADJECTIVES & ADVERBS

ADJECTIVE & ADVERB CHART

Name_____

Page	Perfect Score	My Score	Page	Perfect Score	My Score
1	22		22	13	
2	40		23	20	
3	18		24	42	
4	36		25	35	
5	19		26	13	
6	34		27	24	
7	83		28	13	
8	75		29	Will vary	
9	87		30	24	
10	38		31	28	
11	76		32	58	
12	40		33	27	
13	30		34	13	
14	26		35	10	
15	19		36	21	
16	18		37	12	
17	18		38	8	
18	18		39	10	
19	38		40	27	
20	24		41	32	
21	12		42	16	

Award

_____

has completed all the adjective
and adverb activities and has
done a super job!

_____   _____
Teacher   Date

Certificate

To _____

For completing the
Adjective and Adverb Book
Congratulations!

_____   _____
Teacher   Date

Name_____

> **An adjective is a describing word. It tells about (modifies) a noun or pronoun.**
> **Adjectives tell either <u>what kind</u>, <u>which one(s)</u>, or <u>how many</u>.**
>
> | | <u>adjective</u> | <u>noun</u> | |
> |---|---|---|---|
> | **Example:** | cold | drink | **(what kind)** |
> | | that | book | **(which one(s))** |
> | | ten | dollars | **(how many)** |

The adjective in each word group has been underlined. Decide which of these questions the adjective answers: how many? which one(s) ? or what kind? Write the answer on the line.

Example: <u>that</u> student **(which one(s))**

1.	<u>freckled</u> face	_____	9.	<u>juicy</u> orange	_____
2.	<u>six</u> days	_____	10.	<u>few</u> people	_____
3.	<u>cruel</u> joke	_____	11.	<u>sharp</u> turn	_____
4.	<u>this</u> desk	_____	12.	<u>these</u> pencils	_____
5.	<u>dill</u> pickle	_____	13.	<u>ragged</u> clothes	_____
6.	<u>plastic</u> fork	_____	14.	<u>eight</u> months	_____
7.	<u>several</u> weeks	_____	15.	<u>no</u> dogs	_____
8.	<u>those</u> dresses	_____	16.	<u>thirsty</u> child	_____

On a separate sheet of paper, write six sentences that contain adjectives that tell: <u>what kind</u>.

Adjectives are words that help you describe and imagine scenes. Adjectives can describe such things as sound, size, taste, touch, smell, appearance, and feelings.

ADJECTIVES

worried	cute	prickly	fuzzy	noisy
little	tired	bumpy	shiny	bitter
silent	tall	big	misty	spicy
shrill	loud	quiet	silly	huge
delicious	sweet	sour	large	ugly
cold	wet	nervous	foolish	shy

Decide to which group each adjective in the box could belong. Write the adjective in the correct column.

SOUND	SIZE	SMELL/TASTE
_____	_____	_____
_____	_____	_____
_____	_____	_____
_____	_____	_____
_____	_____	_____

TOUCH	APPEARANCE	FEELINGS
_____	_____	_____
_____	_____	_____
_____	_____	_____
_____	_____	_____
_____	_____	_____

On a separate sheet of paper, write sentences using 10 of the adjectives above.

2

List some of the nouns that you see in the pictures.
Use an adjective to describe each noun.

ADJECTIVE	NOUN
_____	_____
_____	_____
_____	_____
_____	_____
_____	_____

On a separate sheet of paper, write six sentences using the adjective-noun combinations above.

Name_____

Write an adjective before each noun below.

Example: <u>shaggy</u> dog   <u>third</u> grade

1. _____ cat	16. _____ flies
2. _____ shoes	17. _____ river
3. _____ leaves	18. _____ lion
4. _____ sun	19. _____ sky
5. _____ house	20. _____ boy
6. _____ sister	21. _____ taxi
7. _____ color	22. _____ duck
8. _____ music	23. _____ apple
9. _____ class	24. _____ breeze
10. _____ bag	25. _____ flame
11. _____ hats	26. _____ tiger
12. _____ tree	27. _____ crowds
13. _____ men	28. _____ cave
14. _____ shirt	29. _____ chair
15. _____ rug	30. _____ cup

On a separate sheet of paper, write six sentences using one of the adjective-noun combinations above in each.

Adjectives & Adverbs   4   ©Remedia Publications 1981, 1995

Underline the adjective in each word group below.

yellow ribbon
secret spot
cracked mirror

beautiful waterfall
white seashell
several months

severe storm
heavy rainfall
sprained ankle

Write a sentence for each word group in parentheses. Underline the adjective in each sentence.

1. (two tickets) _____

_____

2. (hot sun) _____

_____

3. (empty bottles) _____

_____

4. (this bicycle) _____

_____

5. (red shoes) _____

_____

6. (several people) _____

_____

7. (brick house) _____

_____

8. (buried treasure) _____

_____

9. (three dogs) _____

_____

10. (large house) _____

_____

The words <u>a</u>, <u>an</u>, and <u>the</u> are a special type of adjective called <u>articles</u>.
There are two types of articles: <u>specific</u> and <u>indefinite</u>.

Example: Hand me **<u>the</u>** paper.   Hand me **<u>a</u>** paper.
(a specific paper)   **(any paper)**

Underline the special adjectives called articles in the sentences below.

1.   The farmer planted an apple tree.
2.   The river rushed through the canyon.
3.   A large eagle soared through the sky.
4.   An elegant lady answered the door.
5.   A large stallion galloped across the field.

When using an indefinite article, use **<u>a</u>** before a word beginning with a
consonant sound and **<u>an</u>** before a word beginning with a vowel sound.

Write <u>a</u> or <u>an</u> in the blank.

1.	_____ ribbon	11.	_____ table
2.	_____ owl	12.	_____ idea
3.	_____ astronaut	13.	_____ pillow
4.	_____ banana	14.	_____ oyster
5.	_____ desk	15.	_____ lake
6.	_____ umbrella	16.	_____ apple
7.	_____ error	17.	_____ farm
8.	_____ truck	18.	_____ egg
9.	_____ orange	19.	_____ clock
10.	_____ rug	20.	_____ elephant

Write a sentence for each of the following word groups: a broken leg, the
poison ivy, an old man, the loud noise. **Underline an adjective in each
sentence.**

**Underline the adjectives in the following sentences.
REMEMBER: The words <u>a</u>, <u>an</u>, and <u>the</u> are adjectives.**

Example: <u>The</u> <u>small</u>, <u>red</u> car slid across <u>the</u> <u>slick</u>, <u>icy</u> road.

1. John had a big, fat, brown toad.

2. The large, red hen laid big, white eggs.

3. An old man sat on the green park bench.

4. A huge wave washed over the beautiful sand castle.

5. Brown, yellow, and orange leaves fell off the big oak tree.

6. Big, bright flashes appeared in the stormy sky.

7. Jenny has big, blue eyes and long, blonde hair.

8. Thin pancake batter turns into fat, golden pancakes.

9. The tiny kitten sleeps on a soft, yellow pillow.

10. Do you want chocolate cake or strawberry pie?

11. The jolly, old man made the little children laugh.

12. Dad bought me a bright, shiny, new bicycle.

13. A sunny day is better than a dark, gloomy day.

14. We made crisp, fried chicken, creamy potato salad, and hot, spicy beans to take to the family picnic.

15. Chocolate chip cookies and ice cold milk make a great bedtime treat!

16. I like the red, black, and yellow jellybeans more than the purple ones.

On a separate sheet of paper, use the following words as adjectives in sentences: swift, fancy, petite, immense.

Underline the adjectives in the following sentences.

1. Rich sat in the hot sun and got a painful sunburn.

2. A red, white, and blue flag flew on the tall flagpole.

3. Mother threw the cracked glass into the garbage can.

4. The young boy walked against the cold, stinging wind.

5. A raisin is a dried, wrinkled grape.

6. Mountain goats climbed the steep, icy slopes.

7. Little boys like to jump in mud puddles.

8. Six girls sat in the front row.

9. I wish I had a tall glass of pink lemonade.

10. The blind man carries a white cane.

11. The woman wore a blue suit and black shoes.

12. The children played in a huge, grassy field.

13. I invited six girls and six boys to the birthday party.

14. The birthday presents were wrapped in beautiful, colored paper.

15. The best things often come in small packages.

16. A big plate of cheese would go well with those crispy crackers.

17. The huge building has many, many steps.

18. The tiny butterfly had brown, orange, and yellow spots on its wings.

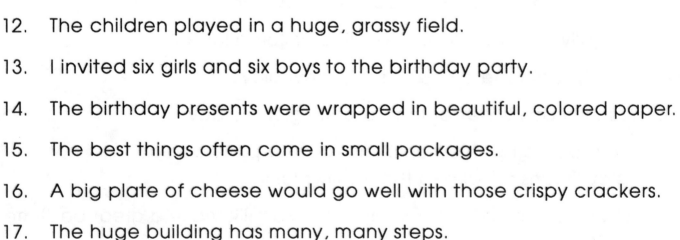

On a separate sheet of paper, use the following words as adjectives in sentences: massive, tasteless, colorful, rapid.

The sentences below contain several adjectives. Circle the nouns in each sentence, then underline the adjectives which modify or describe them.
Example: See <u>that</u> <u>tall</u>, <u>young</u>, <u>handsome</u> (boy.)

1. We have a big, tall, old fir tree in the yard.

2. That sleepy lion looks like a tame cat.

3. A small, brown bat flew from the cave.

4. The new, blue car belongs to him.

5. Those silly, little puppies rolled in the grass.

6. Moldy, green cheese should not be eaten.

7. The little girl stood shivering in wet, dirty,

   dripping clothes.

8. These are lovely, red roses.

9. Look at those pretty, fluffy, white clouds.

10. The young woman poured the old, sour milk down the drain.

11. Look at that big, tall, strong man.

12. We saw a gray, old, ugly house.

13. We used orange, yellow, and red paint on the posters.

14. Before the game, they decorated the gym with three, huge

    pictures of the team and red, white, and yellow streamers.

On a separate sheet of paper, use these words in sentences as adjectives that tell what kind: crying, screeching, screaming, boiling.

Name_____

Write an adjective from the sentence.
Write the noun the adjective modifies
or describes.
Do not write <u>a</u>, <u>an</u>, or <u>the</u>.

	ADJECTIVE	**NOUN**
Example: Jenny cleaned the messy room.	**messy**	**room**

	ADJECTIVE	**NOUN**
1. We ate a quick lunch	_____	_____
2. Most people like TV.	_____	_____
3. I read five stories.	_____	_____
4. We like our new house.	_____	_____
5. That fence needs painting.	_____	_____
6. I painted this picture.	_____	_____
7. Few people like spiders.	_____	_____
8. We jogged three miles.	_____	_____
9. A truck towed the old car.	_____	_____
10. We entered the dark room.	_____	_____
11. The cracked mirror fell.	_____	_____
12. The large dog ran fast.	_____	_____
13. The little boy was lost.	_____	_____
14. The lady has a straw purse.	_____	_____
15. Several people went to the meeting.	_____	_____
16. We saw a mountain goat.	_____	_____
17. Jane has a pair of diamond earrings.	_____	_____

**On a separate sheet of paper, use the following words as adjectives in
sentences:** this, that, these, those.

Twenty of the words in the box below can be adjectives. Underline the words that could tell <u>what kind</u>, <u>which one(s)</u>, or <u>how many</u> about something.

dirty	these	are	but	cute	tall	that
stove	young	ugly	have	this	shiny	pretty
dark	quickly	and	seven	several	first	every
four	could	sharp	did	bushy	short	smart

The words below can be described. For each letter in the word, write an adjective that tells <u>what kind</u>, <u>which one(s)</u>, or <u>how many</u> about the word.

B _____   M _____   L _____

U _____   E _____   A _____

G _____   N _____   D _____

                                                         Y _____

T _____   F _____   D _____

E _____   R _____   O _____

A _____   I _____   G _____

C _____   E _____

H _____   N _____

E _____   D _____

R _____

List four things the following adjectives could describe.

gigantic   _____   _____   _____   _____

beautiful   _____   _____   _____   _____

straight   _____   _____   _____   _____

Look around the classroom. Write the names of six objects you see. After each object, write two adjectives.

Name_____

Adjectives do not always come before the noun they describe.
Sometimes they come after a verb of being (am, is, are, was, were,
be, being, been). Sometimes they come after a verb of the senses
(seems, tastes, looks, smells, feels, etc.).

In each sentence below, underline the adjective that comes <u>after</u> the
verb. On the line, write the adjective before the noun it describes
or modifies.

Example: The sky is <u>**cloudy**</u>.   <u>**cloudy sky**</u>

1.   The view is beautiful. _____

2.   Chimpanzees are smart. _____

3.   The airport was busy. _____

4.   The party was delightful. _____

5.   My milk tastes sour. _____

6.   The carpet feels wet. _____

7.   Your puppy looks sad. _____

8.   The meal will be expensive. _____

9.   This food may be cold. _____

10. The music seemed loud. _____

11. Dad's memory is excellent. _____

12. The wood feels smooth. _____

13. Your dinner looks good. _____

14. A desert is hot. _____

15. The circus was exciting. _____

16. That class can be boring. _____

17. This fog is thick. _____

18. The astronaut was brave. _____

**On a separate sheet of paper, use the following words as adjectives in
sentences:** young, old, gigantic, short. **Place the adjective after the verb.**

Name_____

Underline the adjectives in the paragraph below.
Do not underline a, an, or the.

    This store has fine vegetables and delicious fruit. These big, red tomatoes will make a good salad. I'll take two pounds. These purple grapes are sweet and juicy. We will want several bunches. That green, leafy lettuce is crisp and fresh. I'll pick out ten, ripe, yellow bananas. The second melon in the row is the biggest. It is huge! Let's select a nice, ripe, prickly pineapple for an afternoon snack. I think we have enough produce for many days.

Write the adjectives you have found above under the correct heading.

WHAT KIND

_____

_____

_____

_____

_____

_____

_____

_____

_____

_____

_____

_____

HOW MANY

_____

_____

_____

_____

_____

WHICH ONE(S)

_____

_____

_____

_____

_____

Underline the adjectives in the paragraph below. Do not underline a, an, or the.

   The pet show is noisy. Those dogs are loud. We saw two beautiful parrots and several colorful parakeets. Look at this gorgeous Persian cat. Some animals are sleeping. How can they sleep with all that noise? A few snakes are here. At least the snakes are quiet. The rabbits have soft, silky fur. These hamsters are fat. Did you see the little, gray mouse bite the large, white rat? The pet show is a lively event.

Write the adjectives you have underlined under the correct headings.

<u>WHAT KIND</u>	<u>HOW MANY</u>
_____	_____
_____	_____
_____	_____
_____	_____
_____	_____
_____	<u>WHICH ONE(S)</u>
_____	_____
_____	_____
_____	_____
_____	_____
_____	
_____	

14

> **Adjectives can be formed by adding the ending y or ly to a noun.
> Example: week   weekly**

In the blank, write the adjective that can be formed from the noun in parentheses.
>   **Example:**   the **dirty** windows **(dirt)**

1.   cold, _____ day (wind)

2.   _____, little boy (sleep)

3.   a _____ stranger (friend)

4.   his _____ payment (month)

5.   black, _____ hair (bush)

6.   big, _____ paw (fur)

7.   wet, _____ road (mud)

8.   a _____ gadget (hand)

9.   my _____ allowance (week)

10. some _____ popcorn (salt)

11. dark, _____ day (cloud)

12. the _____ gravy (lump)

13. a _____ mood (grouch)

14. small, _____ puppies (fuzz)

On a separate sheet of paper, use five of the phrases above in sentences.

> **Adjectives can be formed by adding <u>ous</u> to a noun.**
> **When the noun ends in <u>y</u>, change the <u>y</u> to <u>i</u> and add <u>ous</u>.**
> **Example: humor   humorous   glory   glorious**

In the blank, write the adjective that can be formed from the noun in parentheses.

Example: black, **<u>poisonous</u>** liquid **(poison)**

1.   the _____ stranger (mystery)

2.   a _____ vacation (marvel)

3.   sharp, _____ curve (danger)

4.   large, _____ bull (fury)

5.   huge, _____ mansion (luxury)

6.   the _____ applause (thunder)

7.   that _____ girl (envy)

8.   the _____ team (victory)

9.   a _____ joke (humor)

10.   beautiful, _____ country (mountain)

11.   the _____ group (harmony)

12.   smart, _____ girl (study)

On a separate sheet of paper, use six of the phrases above in sentences.

Adjectives can be formed by adding <u>ed</u> or <u>ing</u> to a verb.
Example: chop   chopped   laugh   laughing

In the blank, write the adjective that can be formed from the verb in parentheses.
        Example: a <u>**rocking**</u> chair **(rock)**

1. dangerous, _____ animals (cage)

2. finely _____ onions (chop)

3. loud, _____ noise (howl)

4. old, _____ mirror (crack)

5. big, _____ fire (crackle)

6. broken, _____ machine (wash)

7. large, _____ saucer (fly)

8. badly _____ fender (dent)

9. my _____ back (ache)

10. the _____ gun (load)

11. the strange, _____ noise (rattle)

12. nicely _____ pants (press)

On a separate sheet of paper, use six of the phrases above in sentences.

17   Adjectives & Adverbs

**In the following story, some of the adjectives
have been underlined. Read the story.**

The children were <u>excited</u> about going to the carnival. Joe was
<u>eager</u> to ride the <u>giant</u> Tilt-a-Whirl. He had a <u>happy</u> smile when he got
into the <u>swaying</u> seat, but he was dizzy and ill when he came off the
<u>whirling</u> ride.

Karen got <u>sticky</u> cotton candy on her face and used a <u>damp</u> napkin to wipe it off.

Bruce was <u>frightened</u> on the <u>big</u> ferris wheel, but Betty was <u>brave</u>
and calm. The children were <u>thirsty</u>, so they each bought a <u>large</u> cup
of <u>cold</u> orange juice., The <u>wavy</u> mirrors in the <u>fun</u> house made their
bodies look <u>strange</u>. They were tired when they left the <u>noisy</u> carnival.

**In the paragraph above, find the underlined adjective that modifies
each of the nouns below. Write it in the space.**

_____ children   _____ Joe

_____ Tilt-a-Whirl   _____ smile

_____ seat   _____ ride

_____ candy   _____ napkin

_____ Bruce   _____ ferris wheel

_____ Betty   _____ children

_____ cup   _____ juice

_____ mirrors   _____ house

_____ bodies   _____ carnival

To show comparison <u>between two things</u>,
adjectives of one or two syllables add <u>er</u>.
Example: short   shorter

When a one-syllable adjective ends in a single consonant
preceded by a single vowel, double the consonant before
adding <u>er</u>.
Example: fat   fatter

An adjective which ends in <u>y</u> changes the <u>y</u> to <u>i</u> before
adding <u>er</u>.
Example: early   earlier

Write the correct form to show comparison between two things.

hot _____	mad _____	smooth_____
thin _____	heavy _____	soft _____
busy _____	dim _____	weak _____
lazy _____	dry _____	dirty _____
large _____	tough _____	crazy _____
slim _____	husky _____	little _____
easy _____	flat _____	sloppy _____
cheap_____	bumpy _____	small _____
fast _____	sad _____	ugly _____
happy_____	sturdy _____	pretty _____

Use eight of the words you have written above in sentences.

To show comparison <u>among three or more things</u>,
adjectives of one or two syllables add <u>est</u>.
Example: short   shortest

When a one-syllable adjective ends in a single consonant preceded
by a single vowel, double the consonant before adding <u>est</u>.
Example: fat   fattest

An adjective which ends in <u>y</u> changes the <u>y</u> to *i* before adding <u>est</u>.
Example: early   earliest

Write the correct form to show comparison among three things.

busy	busier	————	soft	softer	————
hot	hotter	————	dirty	dirtier	————
easy	easier	————	bright	brighter	————
sad	sadder	————	lazy	lazier	————
sweet	sweeter	————	warm	warmer	————
heavy	heavier	————	sloppy	sloppier	————
dry	drier	————	steep	steeper	————
husky	huskier	————	wide	wider	————
bumpy	bumpier	————	quick	quicker	————
flat	flatter	————	windy	windier	————

Write sentences containing the following forms: nicer, neater, slimmest,
silliest.

20

> To show comparison <u>between two things</u>, some adjectives
> of two or more syllables add the word <u>more</u>.
> Example: That was terrible.   This is <u>more</u> terrible.

Fill in each blank with an adjective of comparison.

1.   This is embarrassing.

     What you did is _____.

2.   Tom's car was expensive.

     Jim's car was _____ .

3.   My bread is delicious.

     Your bread is _____.

4.   The math test was difficult.

     The science test was _____.

5.   The bracelet Is valuable.

     The necklace is _____.

6.   My friends are important.

     My family is _____.

7.   The book was interesting.

     The movie was _____.

8.   The vice-president is famous.

     The president is _____.

Write sentences containing the following forms: more unfriendly, more
serious, more expensive, more crowded.

Name_____

> To show comparison among <u>three or more things</u>, some adjectives of two or more syllables add the word <u>most</u>.
> Example: beautiful   more beautiful   <u>most</u> beautiful

Fill in each blank with the correct adjective of comparison.

1. wonderful   more wonderful   _____
2. useful   more useful   _____
3. intelligent   more intelligent   _____
4. delicious   more delicious   _____
5. valuable   more valuable   _____
6. important   more important   _____

Fill in each blank with the correct adjective of comparison.

1. I am bashful.

    My sister is more bashful.

    My brother is the _____.

2. History is difficult.

    English is more difficult.

    Math is the _____.

3. Sandy is attractive.

    Susan is more attractive.

    Sally is the _____.

Write sentences containing the following forms: more important, most important, more delicious, most delicious.

**A few adjectives don't follow the rules when forming comparisons.
Instead, the entire word changes.**

Example:	To compare two	To compare three or more
good	better	best
bad	worse	worst

Write good, better, or best in the blanks below.

1. James is a _____ bowler.

2. Ted is a _____ bowler than James.

3. Of all three, David is the _____ bowler.

4. My sister had a _____ idea, but I had a
   _____ one.

5. Ted is a _____ singer than Kevin.

6. Jack was the _____ student in the class.

7. Of the two girls, Tammy is the _____ dancer.

8. Of the three boys, Mike is the _____ dancer.

Write bad, worse, or worst in the blanks below.

1. We have had several _____ storms this year.

2. Of the two storms this month, today's storm was _____.

3. In fact, today's storm was the _____ so far.

4. This year's weather is _____ than last year's weather.

5. Joe has a _____ cold.

6. Joe's sister has a _____ cold than Joe.

7. This is the _____ sentence in the book.

On a separate sheet of paper, write sentences for each of the follow-ing words: better, best, worse, worst.

Write the forms that compare for each of the adjectives below.

		COMPARING TWO	COMPARING THREE OR MORE
1.	smart	_____	_____
2.	famous	_____	_____
3.	little	_____	_____
4.	bad	_____	_____
5.	lonely	_____	_____
6.	lucky	_____	_____
7.	pleasant	_____	_____
8.	good	_____	_____
9.	careful	_____	_____
10.	wonderful	_____	_____
11.	silly	_____	_____
12.	funny	_____	_____
13.	fantastic	_____	_____
14.	happy	_____	_____
15.	sad	_____	_____
16.	bright	_____	_____
17.	dull	_____	_____
18.	easy	_____	_____

Write sentences containing the following forms: more beautiful, more careful, most wonderful, worse, best, funniest.

Name_____

Adjectives can modify pronouns as well as nouns.

**Underline adjectives in the sentences below. In the
blank, write the pronouns that the adjective or adjectives modify.**
    Example: It is <u>cloudy</u> and <u>rainy</u>.   <u>It</u>

1. It is salty and bitter.   _____

2. I am happy today.   _____

3. He was naughty and selfish.   _____

4. Before the game, she was nervous and tense.   _____

5. They were tired.   _____

6. After the rain, it was cool outside.   _____

7. They played long and were tired and hungry.   _____

8. She dropped her glass, and it was broken.   _____

9. Tom stayed up all night, and he was sleepy.   _____

10. Looking over the edge, we were dizzy.   _____

11. The winner looked like he was happy.   _____

12. She is the youngest of the three sisters.   _____

13. The house is old, and it is gray and ugly.   _____

**On separate sheet of paper, use each of the following words as
adjectives in sentences:** brick, plaid, broken, clean.

Some adjectives must be spelled with a capital letter because they are formed from proper nouns. When a proper adjective is formed from a proper noun, the spelling is changed.
Example: Italy   Italian

PROPER ADJECTIVES FORMED FROM PROPER NOUNS

France--French   Canada--Canadian   Egypt--Egyptian
England--English   Germany--German   Denmark--Danish
China--Chinese   Switzerland--Swiss   Brazil--Brazilian
Ireland--Irish   Alaska--Alaskan   Mexico--Mexican
Spain--Spanish   Japan--Japanese   India--Indian
Africa--African   Rome--Roman   Hawaii--Hawaiian

Write each adjective that comes from the noun given in parentheses.

1.   I bought a (Switzerland) _____ watch.

2.   We ordered (France) _____ onion soup.

3.   Do you speak the (England) _____ language?

4.   I like (Germany) _____potato salad.

5.   We saw an (Egypt) _____ mummy.

6.   The sled was pulled by an (Alaska) _____ husky.

7.   Have you ever seen a (Mexico) _____jumping bean?

8.   There is a song titled "When (Ireland) _____ Eyes are Smiling."

9.   Do you like (Hawaii) _____ music?

10. Spaghetti is an (Italy) _____ dish.

Use each of the following word groups in a sentence: Idaho potatoes, California oranges, Irish stew. **Underline the proper adjective in each of your sentences.**

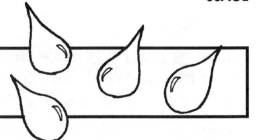

Adjectives can make sentences more meaningful and interesting.

Fill in each blank with an adjective that answers the question underneath the blank.

Example: <u>Several</u> <u>huge</u> drops of rain fell on my face.
How many?   What size?

1. _____ _____ dogs ran across the yard.
    How many?   What kind?

2. The _____ lady wore a _____ dress.
        What kind?   What color?

3. Tara put the _____ , _____ necklace in a
                  What size?   What kind?

    _____ , _____ box.
    What shape?   What color?

4. We saw a _____ , _____ bear standing
              What size?   What color?

    beside the _____ tree.
               What kind?

5. Andy wore a _____ coat and _____ pants.
                What kind?   What kind?

6. The _____ , _____ man yelled at the
        What kind?   What kind?

    _____ _____ boys.
    How many?   What kind?

7. The _____ _____ kittens drank milk.
        How many?   What kind?

Use these words in sentences as adjectives that tell what kind:
favorite, gold, kitchen, high, green.

Place two or more adjectives in the blanks.
**Remember: Words like a, an, the, some, that, this,
those, and these are adjectives.**

Example:
_____ actress waved to _____ crowd.
The beautiful, young actress waved to **the huge, excited** crowd.

1.   _____ boy was chased by _____

       _____ dogs.

2.   I bought _____ dress, _____

       shoes, and _____ purse.

3.   We saw _____ man with _____

       _____ beard.

4.   _____ leaves began to fall from _____

       _____ trees.

5.   The _____ woman ran after the _____

       _____ boy.

6.   _____ rock star put on a _____

       _____ concert.

7.   We watched the _____ birds fly across _____

       _____ lake.

8.   _____ flowers grew beside the _____

       _____ fence.

9.   _____ apples grew on the _____

       _____ tree.

Use these words in sentences as adjectives that tell how many: six,
several, some, twenty.

Rewrite the stories below. Add adjectives to describe the underlined nouns in each story.

One <u>day</u>, a <u>lady</u> began to cross the <u>street</u>. She didn't see the <u>truck</u>. A <u>boy</u> yelled at her just in time. The <u>lady</u> jumped back. The boy's <u>voice</u> had saved her life.

_____

_____

_____

_____

_____

_____

_____

The <u>man</u> threw open the <u>door</u> of the <u>bank</u>. He was carrying a <u>sack</u>.   He jumped into a car and the <u>driver</u> sped away. Two <u>policemen</u> jumped into a <u>car</u> and began chasing the <u>robbers</u>. You could hear the <u>sound</u> of the siren as they raced down the <u>street</u>.

_____

_____

_____

_____

_____

_____

Adverbs tell something about verbs, adjectives, or other adverbs.
They tell <u>how</u>, <u>when</u>, or <u>where</u>.
Example: The girl crossed the street **carefully**. (how)
We traveled to New York **recently**. (when)
The train moved **forward**. (where)

quickly	today	downtown
soon	here	easily
down	slowly	carefully
sadly	then	tomorrow
yesterday	quietly	finally
upstairs	lately	anywhere
late	now	outside
everywhere	always	closer

Words in the box above can be adverbs. Look at each word. Decide whether the word tells <u>how</u>, <u>when</u>, or <u>where</u>. Write the word in the proper column.

HOW	WHEN	WHERE
_____	_____	_____
_____	_____	_____
_____	_____	_____
_____	_____	_____
_____	_____	_____
_____	_____	_____
_____	_____	_____
_____	_____	_____
_____	_____	_____

30

Name_____

An adverb can sometimes be formed by adding <u>ly</u> to an adjective.
When the adjective ends in <u>y</u>, change the <u>y</u> to <u>i</u> before adding <u>ly</u>.
Example: happy   happily

In the blanks, write the adverb formed from the adjective.

1.	slow	_____	16	light	_____
2.	sharp	_____	17.	easy	_____
3.	graceful	_____	18.	sad	_____
4.	smooth	_____	19.	lucky	_____
5.	dangerous	_____	20.	merry	_____
6.	careful	_____	21.	speedy	_____
7.	neat	_____	22.	fresh	_____
8.	quick	_____	23.	bright	_____
9.	sure	_____	24.	greedy	_____
10.	sudden	_____			
11.	tearful	_____			
12.	loud	_____			
13.	rough	_____			
14.	late	_____			
15.	soft	_____			

**On a separate sheet of paper, use the following words in sentences as
adverbs that tell <u>when</u>:** finally, then, later, early.

Adverbs can tell <u>how</u>, <u>when</u>, or <u>where</u>
the action of the verb happens.

Circle the adverb in each phrase. On the line, write whether the
adverb tells <u>how</u>, <u>when</u>, or <u>where</u> something happens.
Example: listen (carefully) <u>how</u>

drives slowly	_____	sit anywhere	_____
played outside	_____	soon learn	_____
arrived today	_____	dress warmly	_____
returned later	_____	yelled loudly	_____
works quickly	_____	moved closer	_____
runs fast	_____	live here	_____
sing softly	_____	moved away	_____
quickly ate	_____	leave soon	_____
left yesterday	_____	finally come	_____
meet again	_____	rained today	_____
felt well	_____	rose higher	_____
comes daily	_____	eats slowly	_____

**Write 10 sentences using one of the verb-adverb combinations above
in each.**

**Read each sentence. On the lines below the sentence, write the verb
and adverb that appear in the sentence. In the box, write whether the
adverb tells <u>how</u>, <u>when</u>, or <u>where</u> something happened.**

Example: Tony finished his work quickly | how |
          (verb) finished   (adverb) quickly

1.   The boys looked everywhere.

     (verb)_____   (adverb)_____

2.   Our paper comes daily.

     (verb)_____ (adverb)_____

3.   John crossed the street carefully.

     (verb)_____ (adverb)_____

4.   The clock ticked loudly.

     (verb)_____ (adverb)_____

5.   I left my coat there.

     (verb)_____ (adverb)_____

6.   The children played outside.

     (verb)_____ (adverb)_____

7.   I took a test today.

     (verb)_____ (adverb)_____

8.   Sometimes I help my mom.

     (verb)_____ (adverb)_____

9.   Our team played badly.

     (verb)_____ (adverb)_____

Rewrite the sentences below, replacing the

star ☆ **with a correct adverb from the box.**

Example: Andy worked his math problems ☆ .
Andy worked his math problems **correctly**.

angrily	bitterly	rudely	mysteriously
blindly	correctly	safely	anxiously

1. The mad bull charged across the field ☆ . _____

_____

2. We crossed the street ☆ . _____

_____

3. If you answer ☆ , you'll win the prize. _____

_____

4. The boy spoke ☆ to his teacher. _____

_____

5. Ann's books disappeared ☆ . _____

_____

6. The woman waited ☆ in the hospital hall. _____

_____

7. David ran ☆ through the storm. _____

_____

8. The man and his son argued ☆ . _____

_____

Use these words in sentences as adverbs that tell <u>when</u>: always,
now, soon, today, tomorrow.

Name_____

Write a sentence for each adverb below.

1. (carefully)   _____

    _____

2. (accidentally) _____

    _____

3. (anxiously)   _____

    _____

4. (noisily)   _____

    _____

5. (quickly)   _____

    _____

6. (silently)   _____

    _____

7. (recklessly)   _____

    _____

8. (sleepily)   _____

    _____

9. (gently)   _____

    _____

10. (nervously)   _____

    _____

Fill in each blank with an adverb. Have the adverb answer the question, HOW?
Example: The policeman looked at the boys **suspiciously**.

1.   Nancy told the story _____.
2.   Randy walked to the office _____.
3.   Please drive _____.
4.   The cat crept _____ toward the mouse.
5.   Keep your voice low. Don't talk _____.

Fill in each blank with an adverb. Have the adverb answer the question: WHERE?
Example: The papers flew **everywhere**.

1.   The children are playing _____.
2.   My dog ran _____.
3.   The bus stops _____.
4.   A wind blew the leaves _____.
5.   The balloon rose _____.

Fill in each blank with an adverb. Have the adverb answer the question: WHEN?
Example: I'll finish my homework **later**.

1.   I'll call you _____.
2.   _____, I remember.
3.   We will eat _____.
4.   I will walk my dog _____.
5.   School will begin _____.

On a separate sheet of paper, write six adverbs that tell _where_. Write a sentence for each adverb you have written.

36

**Rewrite the sentences below, replacing the words in parentheses with
the correct adverb from the box.**

Example: The puppy ate its food **(in a greedy way)**.
                         The puppy ate its food **greedily**.

silently	equally	correctly	Luckily
carelessly	thoughtfully	often	daily

1.   Our family eats in a cafe (very many times).

        _____

2.   My sister and I share chores (so we each have the same number).

        _____

3.   (By good luck), the puppy was not hit by the car.

        _____

4.   Cindy was able to answer the questions (with no mistakes).

        _____

5.   We receive a newspaper (every day).

        _____

6.   The boys sat (with no noise) waiting for the principal.

        _____

7.   Mark (in a thoughtful manner) opened the door for his mother.

        _____

8.   You should never walk (without care) across the street.

        _____

Use these words in sentences as adverbs that tell <u>how</u>: smoothly, badly, wisely, safely.

Name_____

Rewrite the sentences below, replacing the words in parentheses with the correct adverb from the box.

Example: Max finished his work **(in a quick way)**.
Max finished his work **quickly**.

purposely	clearly	neatly	eventually
truthfully	accidentally	enormously	annually

1.   The little boy hit his sister (on purpose).

_____

2.   The population of this state increased (in a large way) in the last

two years. _____

_____

3.   Mr. Jackson told his story (without telling a lie).

_____

4.   Our bus arrived (after a long delay).

_____

5.   Tommy dropped his plate (without meaning to).

_____

6.   The principal told the boys (in a clear way) what they must do.

_____

_____

7.   The group has a meeting (once every year).

_____

8.   Mindy arranged the clothes (in a neat and tidy way).

_____

Name_____

In each of the following sentences, an adjective has been underlined. Rewrite each sentence, changing the adjective to an adverb.

Example: Sara was **careful** when she carried the glasses.
Sara carried the glasses **carefully**.

1. Dana was a quick worker.

    _____

2. Brandon was a rapid runner.

    _____

3. Kim was noisy when she came into the library.

    _____

4. Darren was angry when he left.

    _____

5. The baby was a slow walker.

    _____

6. Lucy was selfish when she ate all the cookies.

    _____

7. Frank tied a tight knot.

    _____

8. Alice was honest when she told her story.

    _____

9. The colt walked to its mother in an awkward way.

    _____

10. Pam was polite when she answered her teacher.

    _____

Use the words below in sentences. Then, in each sentence, underline an adverb and circle the verb it modifies.
Example: (dangerous, suddenly)
       A dangerous twister <u>**suddenly**</u> appeared in the sky.

1.   (old, slowly)   _____

     _____

2.   (delicious, often)   _____

     _____

3.   (dirty, finally)   _____

     _____

4.   (skinny, quickly)   _____

     _____

5.   (red, safely)   _____

     _____

6.   (happy, soon)   _____

     _____

7.   (friendly, always)   _____

     _____

8.   (cloudy, usually)   _____

     _____

9.   (huge, suddenly)   _____

     _____

Look for adjectives in your sentences. Write "adj." above each adjective you find.

40

Many adjectives and adverbs have been used in this story. See if you can find and circle 20 adjectives and underline 12 adverbs.

One hot, sunny morning, the Davis family decided to drive to the ocean. They would spend the whole day in the cool water and on the warm, sandy beach. Mrs. Davis prepared a picnic lunch hurriedly and packed it in a big, wicker basket. The children gathered their beach towels, swim suits, and sand toys excitedly. That task took only a few minutes.

The brilliant sun shown brightly on the huge, white waves that crashed noisily on the shore. Everyone looked eagerly toward the inviting, sparkling water. Danny squealed shrilly and dove wildly into a gigantic whitecap. Candice dipped her small foot cautiously into the crawling surf as it washed gently over the sand. Dad swam gracefully with swift, strong strokes toward the deep water. Mrs. Davis spread her beach blanket carefully on the smooth sand and settled down to acquire a golden tan, or maybe a painful sunburn.

Lunch was a welcome meal. Everyone was hungry. Those sandwiches mother made were devoured fast. As the glowing sun set gradually below the faraway, blue horizon, the Davis family picked up their wet towels, sandy blankets, and leftover picnic items wearily and walked slowly to their car for the long ride home.

Write a paragraph to describe something you have seen. It may be a place, a person, an animal, a picture, an event, or something else. Describe it so that someone who has not seen it would know clearly what you are writing about. Use at lest ten adjectives and six adverbs in the paragraph.

ADJECTIVE & ADVERBS- ANSWER KEY

Page 1

1. what kind
2. how many
3. what kind
4. which one
5. what kind
6. what kind
7. how many
8. which ones
9. what kind
10. how many
11. what kind
12. which ones
13. what kind
14. how many
15. how many
16. what kind

Page 2

Sound	Smell/Taste	Appearance
silent	delicious	cute
shrill	sweet	misty
loud	sour	ugly
quiet	bitter	shiny
noisy	spicy	Feeling(s)
Size	**Touch**	worried
little	cold	tired
tall	wet	sore
big	prickly	silly
large	fuzzy	nervous
huge	bumpy	shy
		foolish

Pages 3, 4

Answers will vary.

Page 5

yellow	several
secret	severe
cracked	heavy
beautiful	sprained
white	Sentences will vary

Page 6

1. The an
2. The the
3. A the
4. An the
5. A the

1. a
2. an
3. an
4. a
5. a
6. an
7. an
8. a
9. an
10. a
11. a
12. an
13. a
14. an
15. a
16. an
17. a
18. an
19. a
20. an

Page 7

1. a big fat brown
2. The large red big white
3. An old the green park
4. A huge the beautiful sand
5. Brown yellow orange the big oak.
6. Big bright the stormy
7. big blue long blond
8. Thin pancake fat golden
9. The tiny a soft yellow
10. chocolate strawberry
11. The jolly old the little
12. a bright shiny new
13. A sunny a dark gloomy
14. crisp fried creamy potato hot spicy the family
15. Chocolate chip ice cold a great bedtime
16. the red black yellow the purple

Page 8

1. the hot a painful
2. A red white blue the tall
3. the cracked the garbage
4. The young the cold stinging
5. A a dried wrinkled
6. Mountain the steep icy
7. Little mud

Page 8 (cont.)

8. Six the front
9. a tall pink
10. The blind a white
11. The a blue black
12. The a huge grassy
13. six six the birthday
14. The birthday beautiful colored
15. The best small
16. A big those crispy
17. The huge many many
18. The tiny brown orange yellow

Page 9

1. a big tall old fir (tree) the (yard)
2. That sleepy (lion) a tame (cat)
3. A small brown (bat) the (cave)
4. The new blue (car)
5. Those silly little (puppies) the (grass)
6. Moldy green (cheese)
7. The little (girl) wet dirty dripping (clothes)
8. These lovely red (roses)
9. those pretty fluffy white (clouds)
10. The young (woman) the old sour (milk) the (drain)
11. that big tall strong (man)
12. a gray old ugly (house)
13. orange yellow red (paint) the (posters)
14. the (game) the (gym) three huge (pictures) the (team) red white yellow (streamers)

Page 10

1. quick lunch
2. Most people
3. five stories
4. new house
5. That fence
6. this picture
7. Few people
8. three miles
9. old car
10. dark room
11. cracked mirror
12. large dog
13. little boy
14. straw purse
15. Several people
16. mountain goat
17. diamond earrings

Page 11

dirty	cute	that
dark	this	pretty
four	several	every
these	bushy	smart
young	tall	Remaining
ugly	shiny	answers
sharp	first	will vary.
seven	short	

Page 12

1. beautiful view
2. smart chimpanzees
3. busy airport
4. delightful party
5. sour milk
6. wet carpet
7. sad puppy
8. expensive meal
9. cold food
10. loud music
11. excellent memory
12. smooth wood
13. good dinner
14. hot desert
15. exciting circus
16. boring class
17. thick fog
18. brave astronaut

Page 13

<u>What kind</u>

fine	juicy	biggest
delicious	green	huge
big	leafy	nice
red	crisp	ripe
good	fresh	prickly
purple	ripe	afternoon
sweet	yellow	

<u>How many</u>	<u>Which one(s)</u>
two	This
several	These
ten	These
enough	That
many	second

Page 14

<u>What kind</u>	
pet	white
noisy	pet
loud	lively
beautiful	<u>How many</u>
colorful	two
gorgeous	several
Persian	Some
quiet	all
soft	few
silky	<u>Which one(s)</u>
fat	Those
little	this
gray	that
large	These

Page 15

1. windy
2. sleepy
3. friendly
4. monthly
5. bushy
6. furry
7. muddy
8. handy
9. weekly
10. salty
11. cloudy
12. lumpy
13. grouchy
14. fuzzy

Page 16

1. mysterious
2. marvelous
3. dangerous
4. furious
5. luxurious
6. thunderous
7. envious
8. victorious
9. humorous
10. mountainous
11. harmonious
12. studious

Page 17

1. caged
2. chopped
3. howling
4. cracked
5. crackling
6. washing
7. flying
8. dented
9. aching
10. loaded
11. rattling
12. pressed

Page 18

excited	whirling
giant	damp
swaying	big
sticky	thirsty
frightened	cold
brave	fun
large	noisy
wavy	
strange	
eager	
happy	

PUNCTUATION - ANSWER KEY

Page 19

hotter	drier	sloppier
thinner	tougher	smaller
busier	huskier	uglier
lazier	flatter	prettier
larger	bumpier	
slimmer	sadder	
easier	sturdier	
cheaper	smoother	
faster	softer	
happier	weaker	
madder	dirtier	
heavier	crazier	
dimmer	littler	

Page 20

busiest	softest
hottest	dirtiest
easiest	brightest
saddest	laziest
sweetest	warmest
heaviest	sloppiest
driest	steepest
huskiest	widest
bumpiest	quickest
flattest	windiest

Page 21

1. more embarrassing
2. more expensive
3. more delicious
4. more difficult
5. more valuable
6. more important
7. more interesting
8. more famous

Page 22

1. most wonderful
2. most useful
3. most intelligent
4. most delicious
5. most valuable
6. most important

1. most bashful
2. most difficult
3. most attractive

Page 23

1. good
2. better
3. best
4. good better
5. better
6. best
7. better
8. best

1. bad
2. worse
3. worst
4. worse
5. bad
6. worse
7. worst

Page 24

1. smarter smartest
2. more famous most famous
3. littler littlest
4. worse worst
5. lonelier loneliest
6. luckier luckiest
7. more pleasant most pleasant
8. better best
9. more careful most careful
10. more wonderful most wonderful
11. sillier silliest
12. funnier funniest
13. more fantastic most fantastic
14. happier happiest
15. sadder saddest
16. brighter brightest
17. duller dullest
18. easier easiest

Adjectives & Adverbs

Page 25

1. salty bitter It
2. happy I
3. naughty selfish He
4. nervous tense she
5. tired They
6. cool it
7. tired hungry They
8. broken it
9. sleepy he
10. dizzy we
11. happy he
12. youngest She
13. gray ugly it

Page 26

1. Swiss
2. French
3. English
4. German
5. Egyptian
6. Alaskan
7. Mexican
8. Irish
9. Hawaiian
10. Italian

Page 27 & Page 28

Answers will vary.

Page 29

Stories will vary.

Page 30

How	When	Where
quickly	soon	down
sadly	yesterday	upstairs
slowly	late	everywhere
quietly	today	here
easily	then	downtown
carefully	lately	anywhere
	now	outside
	always	closer
	tomorrow	
	finally	

Page 31

1. slowly
2. sharply
3. gracefully
4. smoothly
5. dangerously
6. carefully
7. neatly
8. quickly
9. surely
10. suddenly
11. tearfully
12. loudly
13. roughly
14. lately
15. softly
16. lightly
17. easily
18. sadly
19. luckily
20. merrily
21. speedily
22. freshly
23. brightly
24. greedily

Page 32

slowly how	soon when
outside where	warmly how
today when	loudly how
later when	closer where
quickly how	here where
fast how	away where
softly how	soon when
quickly how	finally when
yesterday when	today when
again when	higher where
well how	slowly how
daily when	
anywhere where	

Page 33

1. looked everywhere where
2. comes daily when
3. crossed carefully how
4. ticked loudly how
5. left there where
6. played outside where
7. took today when
8. help Sometimes when
9. played badly how

Page 34

1. angrily
2. safely
3. correctly
4. rudely
5. mysteriously
6. anxiously
7. blindly
8. bitterly

Page 35

Sentences will vary.

Page 36

Answers will vary.

Page 37

1. often
2. equally
3. Luckily
4. correctly
5. daily
6. silently
7. thoughtfully
8. carelessly

Page 38

1. purposely
2. enormously
3. truthfully
4. eventually
5. accidentally
6. clearly
7. annually
8. neatly

Page 39

1. Dana worked quickly.
2. Brandon ran rapidly.
3. Kim came into the library noisily.
4. Darren left angrily.
5. The baby walked slowly.
6. Lucy ate all the cookies selfishly.
7. Frank tied a knot tightly.
8. Alice told her story honestly.
9. The colt walked awkwardly to its mother.
10. Pam answered her teacher politely.

Page 40

Sentences will vary.

Page 41

Answers will vary.

Page 42

Paragraphs will vary.

©Remedia Publications 1981, 1995